# Gaia
## Body and Soul

IN HONOUR OF MOTHER EARTH
AND THE FEMININE SPIRIT

# TONI CARMINE SALERNO

BLUE ANGEL® PUBLISHING

*"Gaia: Body and Soul"*

*Published by*
*Blue Angel Publishing®*
*80 Glen Tower Drive, Glen Waverley,*
*Victoria, Australia 3150*
*Email: info@blueangelonline.com*
*Website: www.blueangelonline.com*

*Writings and paintings by Toni Carmine Salerno*

*Edited by Tanya Graham*

*Blue Angel is a registered trademark of Blue Angel Gallery Pty. Ltd.*

*Printed in China*

*ISBN: 978-0-9802865-4-0*

## Sacred Invocation

*One heart — One people*

*My heart — My people*

*A global thought — A global dream*

*I am one with the wind*

*I am one with Gaia*

*Through her eyes*

*Through different eyes*

*Eternal visions*

*One global, universal heart*

*Look into her soul*

*She has a story to tell*

*A beautiful sphere of dreams*

*Through her eyes*

*A vision of the great mother*

*Gaia — the eternal goddess*

# Foreword

In ancient times the world was but a thought – an image in the heart of love.

Long before the dawn of time, a beautiful vision appeared within a particle of light, and the vision was projected from the minds of the Goddesses and Gods that ruled the heavens. The light streamed forth from their hearts and minds and our Universe was born through an explosion of love. The sacred journey began to unfold its sacred path; the path upon which all of creation travels.

A divine imagination gave birth to millions of stars which filled great voids of space, and time began to turn its invisible wheels. One day a star exploded and the love it held within its heart travelled through space and settled as stardust in a galaxy we now call the Milky Way. As the stardust settled, the Earth was formed, and love was the essence of its formation. Gaia, the Goddess of the Earth, appeared from within the heart of the Earth and her spirit flowed through the waters of the Earth and through the trees and valleys, the mountains and the rivers and flowers and permeated the rocks and sand and soil, until the entire planet was infused with her love and wisdom, with her beauty and strength, and with her grace and will. Her will was the will of the Gods and Goddesses that ruled the heavens and so Heaven and Earth merged. Heaven embraced the Earth and the Earth became one with the great cosmic creation that is all there is, and Gaia was revered by humankind. She was honoured and prayed to and held sacred and loved along with the Sun and the Moon and the stars. The Earth was held lovingly in a prism of light within the heart of Gaia.

Eons of time passed and many beautiful stories were written in the book of life…and memories formed in the hearts of humankind. Then one day, the memories began to fade and the people began to forget that they were held within Gaia's loving embrace, along with everything else on the Earth. Because of this, humankind began to experience fear and the people began to feel separate from the Earth and separate from one another and so a whole new story began to unfold and humankind began to create its own version of reality, and through their fears Heaven on Earth often felt like Hell on Earth. With the invention of Hell, love began to fade until Gaia eventually became a distant memory and the people forgot that the Earth was sacred and that all was lovingly held and protected by a prism of light in the heart of Gaia, and for thousands of years thereafter the world experienced much anguish and suffering due to fear and ignorance…

Yet through all this love's light continued to glow – the few became the custodians of the light and held it lovingly for the many.

Until one day, around about this time, the many began to awaken from their slumber and they started to remember…the Earth is sacred – I am one with the Earth and stars – love is forever present in my heart – I am intuitively guided by the great spirit of life – I am safe and my spirit is eternal.

They began to help the Earth, respect and love the Earth, and honour the Earth once more. They rediscovered their souls and started to remember who they truly were. Their awareness of life changed and as their hearts opened, their minds became clear and illuminated and humankind rediscovered the ancient and sacred knowledge that had lain dormant in their hearts and in their hearts they found what they had for so long searched for, and in their hearts they felt Gaia's loving presence and Gaia was pleased and the journey continues….

*Toni Carmine Salerno*

*Before we know it, we will return*
*to the great void from whence we came*
*A moment in time, a pause in the eternal wheel of life,*
*and a new cycle begins*
*A lifetime is simply one moment in eternity*

To love is to feel
To love is to accept all there is as it is
To love is to feel complete
To love is to know that nothing is missing,
For everything is a part of you –
There is no separation
Yet in spite of this, there is sadness in the heart of love
Because love forever yearns,
It forever ebbs and flows between pleasure and pain
Love is both empty and full
In love you get both laughter and tears
Love is the builder and destroyer of our illusions
And beyond this…
Love is all there is

*A heart yearns, a soul ebbs and flows*
*A dream becomes a reality*
*Only to discover that reality is a dream*

# Dreams

**Dreams** can be prophetic or symbolic; in a way they are both. Yet on a higher level there is no such thing as prophecy because prophecy infers that time is real and in actuality it is not, at least not as we perceive it. Time is an invisible wheel that turns our imagination and takes us on a journey through an already existing path. Therefore, prophecy is like reading a book; the story was written well before you begin to read. Prophecy is simply the ability to foresee the pages that one has not yet read, but it is not an ability to foretell the future.

*The imaginary wheels of time –*
*the immortal present moment*

*Your* thoughts,

feelings and intentions

are living energies.

In a way, thoughts are life's conduits

that carry your feelings and intentions

until they manifest as your physical reality.

Therefore, observe your thoughts,

monitor your feelings

and be sure of your intentions.

Then ask yourself,

"Is this what I want to create?"

If it is, then good,

if it isn't then all you need to do

is change your thoughts so that they align

with your true intentions.

Feel that which you wish to be,

create in the sanctuary of your heart

and bathe your dreams in love.

*On* a dark velvet night the Goddess dreams
Luminous visions of love that reflect the light of the Moon
Luna smiles and the universe whispers
And a stream of light pours forth from her most sacred heart

Luna smiles and the sky whispers with a gentle breeze
That blows through my thoughts and illuminates my soul
In the sanctuary of her heart I am safe
Through light beams and dreams she guides me to the centre
Where her heartfelt truth is revealed…

Seek not forgiveness, for you are your only judge
You are the way
You are the dream beyond the meadow
Beyond the veil
Beyond this world of illusion
There is an otherworld
A dreamtime beyond this one
Where the Luna and the Sun, united through love,
Give birth to a new day
Through which another universe is born

The dark velvet night of the soul . . .

# AUTUMN MEDITATION

Imagine yourself in a beautiful park on a sunny autumn day.

Above you a clear blue sky — and you are surrounded by beautiful trees and lush green fields scattered with autumn leaves that gently fall around you creating a carpet of yellow, gold, crimson, red and purple.

Feel a golden ray of sunlight streaming down through the trees as you close your eyes and relax into a profound sense of peace and tranquillity. Feel the Earth beneath you, feel Gaia's heart beat, her warmth, strength and love. Aware of her ancient and timeless wisdom, each breath you breathe fills you with light and only love surrounds you.

You feel a deep sense of peace. You are now one with the light, and all you see and feel is love. A five-pointed star appears within your heart centre. You are a sacred star within the sanctuary of Mother Earth.

# Through love

all unites eternally
All is one in eternity
Light gives birth to time –
The imaginary time of our imaginary world
Many seasons – one eternal moment
A floating thought creating space –
An imaginary space within a prism of light
Where truth dwells and where it is also distorted
A place in your soul
Where the path is predestined but never predictable
Before you spoke a single word
Long before even a thought of you was born
The eternal fire of love sparkled
In her dreams you were born
Just as the Sun's golden arrow pierced your heart
Now you forever bleed a crimson river
And your nights are forever filled with longing
In the heart of love, a secret is revealed
You are forever transforming into ever-greater light
Her truth is timeless
It transforms you
It created you – the tree of life
With branches reaching for Heaven
And roots penetrating deep into the heart of her soil
The union of Heaven and Earth is born

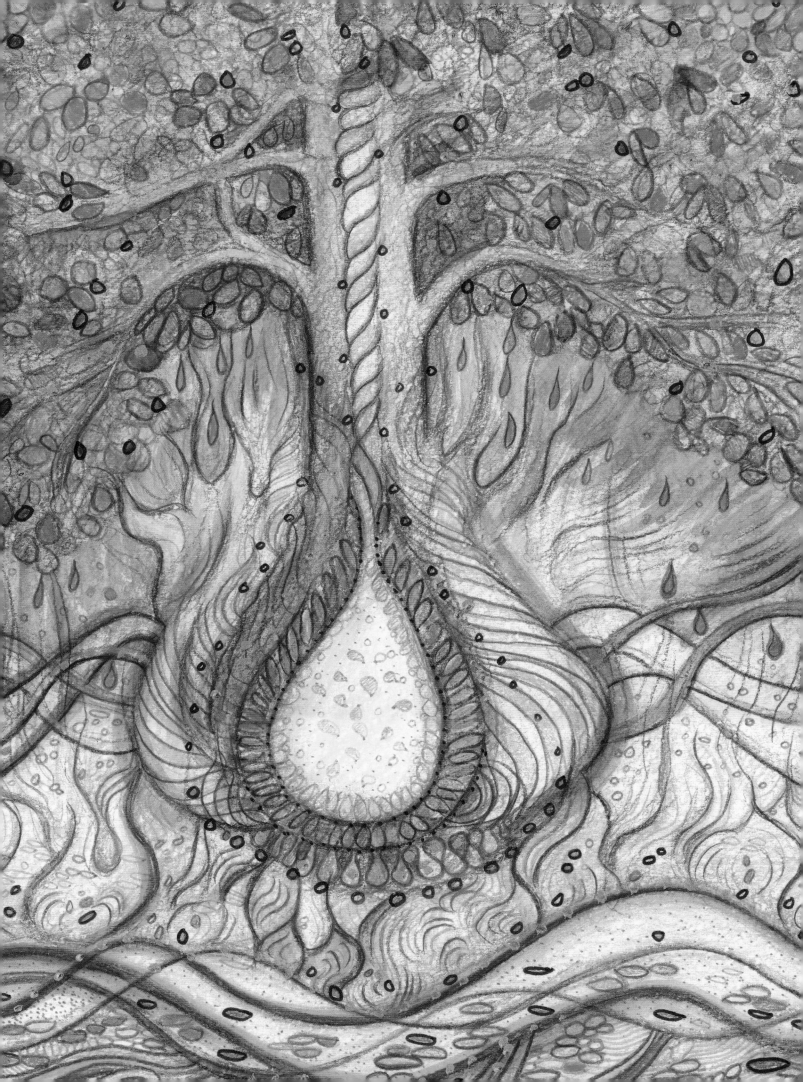

*Tears and laughter*

*are both expressions of love*

**Your** physical form
will one day cease to be,
yet your spirit will continue to live
beyond the horizon of time.

*In time we will all realise*

*that only love is real*

*the eternal light of love …*

*… a gift from her most sacred heart*

Love is a universe forever unfolding
Love forever yearns to fulfil its potential
As it creates and illuminates all things
Love is life in perpetual motion
A journey through the soul of the One
Whose will moves the Earth and stars
A state of grace beyond words or concepts
The builder and destroyer of our dreams
Love is the fire we feel inside us
It is the passion that burns eternally in our hearts
It is a desire to be one with all creation

*We travel through the endless corridors of our mind*

*until one day we find a pathway that leads to our heart.*

Most of the species of life forms
that have ever existed on earth
are presently extinct.
Yet, the total amount of
life has not diminished.
Life on our planet continually
changes form —
When one species dies something
else is born and takes its
place —
    nothing is ever truly lost.
He world doesn't need
saving — it just needs to
be loved —

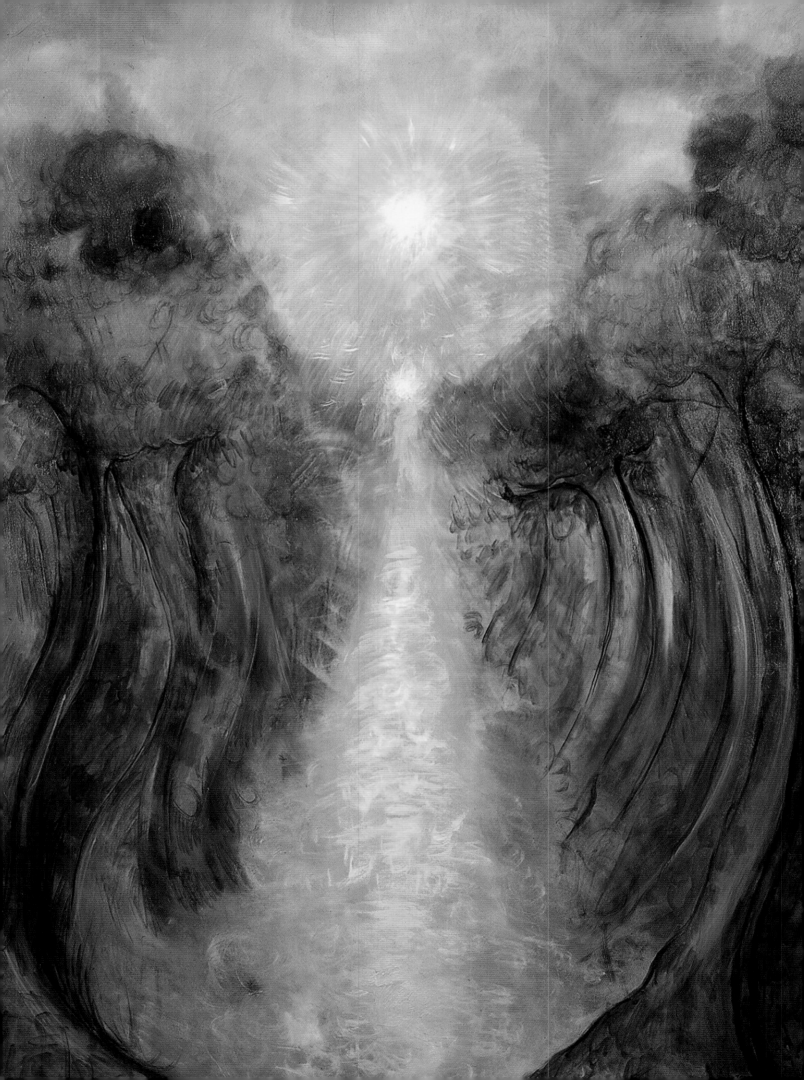

*Imagine* a golden path
Surrounded by lush trees and flowers

The golden path is your life's journey
The sun your soul's guiding light

You are always on this golden path
Whether you know it or not

*Within* the heart of my beloved
There is an eternal light
A memory forever imprinted in the stars
The miracle of love unites us
And together we are one
An eternal thought within the mind of the Sun
One flame
That glows through infinite layers of dreams
Through the will of the one
whose love moves the heavenly stars
A heart filled with infinite longing
The image of eternity reflected throughout the universe
Through every thought, every smile, every whisper
Love is an eternal grace
A gift from the one whose light shone
before the dawn of time
We are one through the gracious light
of the beloved

---

*Heart* and mind
are complimentary opposites
Everything has a positive and a negative aspect
Nothing is just one or the other
Every event and action has both
There is no light without darkness
No warm without cold, no happy without sad,
no joy without pain
You are both positive and negative,
so embrace all of who you are
Positive and negative are soul mates,
one cannot exist without the other

*What* may seem like an undeniable truth to you
may seem false to another.

No one is ever absolutely right or absolutely wrong,
there is no single truth that applies universally.

Every statement one makes can be considered both true and false;
this is because a piece of the truth exists in each point of view.

Therefore, there is little that one can say
with absolute certainty.

The only eternal truth is love,
for love accepts all as it is.

*Try* to imagine what things were like the moment the universe was born.

At some point far back in time, a tiny point of light within the underlying fabric of creation exploded. That explosion has become known as the Big Bang. Unimaginable heat and radiation expanded from a point smaller than an atom to become the enormous ever-expanding universe of today.

This mysterious super-luminous event triggered the seemingly endless cycles of creation and transformation responsible for the present day universe. 'We' — 'The Universe' — continue to expand and evolve through time and space.

Because we are so caught up in our everyday concerns we often forget that we exist on this beautiful planet surrounded by a sea of stars and galaxies that span trillions of light years through space.

If we were to view our life from a higher perspective we would realise that we are but a grain of sand, within a great cosmic ocean of space and stars in a universe driven by a will and intelligence far greater than our own. The energy that emanates from this higher intelligence infuses and energetically links all things.

Remember, we all come from the same place; we are all born from the one point of light. Within this universal energy past, present and future are eternally present. We are all a part of the moving image of eternity.

Prior to our
explosive birth
before the
dawn of time
we and our
entire universe
were but
a speck of light.
Through a
super-luminous
event
we were born
and to this
very day
we remain
in essence light.

This beautiful planet lives eternally within my heart
I am one with the light of the sun
One with the breeze that flows through
from the heart of Gaia

*Be true to yourself.* Even though you will make mistakes along the way, know that these are valuable lessons from which you grow. Create, for it is in creation that you exist, in this world of dreams that stem from the universal heart. You will experience many things along your journey. Love and hatred, joy and sadness, laughter and tears; all are valuable experiences – embrace them.

At times you may find yourself full of fear and doubt. Face your fear and then do it anyway. Your soul will guide you if you let it. It will show you the way if you trust it.

Visualise your dreams; imagine them nourished by the light of the Sun. Go wherever love beckons you, do what you feel you must. You may encounter darkness along the way. If you fear the darkness, it will haunt you. Embrace it and it will transform to light. Be aware that you have a higher and lower mind. The thoughts generated by your lower mind are often limited and fear-based. The thoughts of your higher mind are full of true wisdom and love. It is through an open and grateful heart that the blessings and inspirations that surround you are able to flow to you and crystallise. Know that your creativity has no boundaries apart from those you place upon it. You are limited only by your negative beliefs. Your creativity is most powerful when you express it without judgment, restriction or conscious thought.

It is human nature to seek a logical explanation for things, however, some things can only be understood by the heart. Not everything has a logical explanation, yet just because something can't be proven, doesn't mean that it's not possible.

this present moment is the
only thing that is real

I am —

An empty space that
fills with love everytime
you are aware.

A pool of infinite potential
exists inside your heart

A universe forever unfolding

love forever fulfills it

potential — As it creates
and illuminates all things

*Your intuition*

*is an antenna that
picks up signals,
spiritual data files,
impressions, blueprints,
thoughts and creative
impulses from your
inner universe.*

*Intuition is a bridge
between your physical
and spiritual self.
It transmits information
through feelings,
emotions and thoughts;
these are whispers of the
soul that house your
truth and unique essence.*

*Listen and be guided
by your soul's infinite
love and wisdom.*

*Let go of preconceived
ideas and be present,
feel this moment and
the eternal presence
of the Goddess.*

Magic dwells

in the empty
space

between our

thoughts

allow my light to fill the oceans
of your heart
with love

*Life* is constantly changing
Nothing ever stays the same
Even in stillness something moves
Invisible rays of energy swirling through light
Waves of consciousness that ebb and flow through our thoughts
Life is an idea forever reinventing itself
Forever transforming inside the universal mind
Life is a series of endless worlds inside an eternal flame
A flame woven from light
A world forever aglow
Even in darkness there is light
She creates and destroys
She appears then leaves
Sometimes suddenly, sometimes slowly
Yet she never leaves without a trace
For deep inside our heart her memory remains –
A memory passed on throughout the ages,
A memory of a dawn before time and endless summers,
Of a mystery revealed only by the light of the Moon
She bares her soul when we seek her counsel –
Ask and you shall know
Seek and you shall find
Accept change and all will lovingly transform

You may not always feel loved
Yet know that I love you all the same
Always I have loved you and always you will be loved
When you are sad, I embrace you
We are spiritually connected by invisible rays
By the same flame that glows within each of our hearts
And for this blessing I am eternally grateful
Even if you are sad at times
I know that beyond our suffering something beautiful exists
Something warm and precious that invites all to enter
I follow my heart and it leads me to your door
I enter to be confronted with the most beautiful vision
A universal light full of universal love fills my soul
And my only thought is of you
The Goddess of Compassion melts in my heart
She is, through you, my guiding light

*By facing our fears and accepting them as valid aspects of who we are, we heal and become whole. Instead of swimming against the current, life starts to flow naturally and we realise that most of the stress in our lives is simply the result of our inner fear and turmoil. Fear clouds our ability to think and see clearly, so start to be aware of your thoughts.*

*When you find yourself thinking fear-based thoughts such as 'I should…' or 'I have to…' pause for a moment. Instead of worrying about what you think you should do or have to do, ask yourself this question, 'What is it that I would love to be doing right now?'*

*Transforming Fear = Liberation*

*If* you think that you're not creative, you are wrong.
Creativity is a part of your true nature.
In one form or another you express your creativity
in every moment of every day.
Whether you know it or not, you are a great artist —
no one has any more or less creative energy than you.
It is not your creativity that needs to be unblocked;
it is just your fears and preconditioned ideas that need to be dissolved.
Express what is in your heart, every emotion, without fear or judgment.

*Pay attention* to your thoughts but do not be automatically guided by them, for thoughts are transient things that belong to the realm of time, and as such, they continually shift and change. Think, but listen also to your heart.

*Beyond* the clatter of your mind there is a place of calm; a space between your thoughts that is the gateway to your heart, a space where the eternal wisdom of your soul dwells.

As each chapter
of your life
comes to a close,
remember,
all is held eternally
in your heart
Every ending is a gateway
to a new beginning

# You are the creator

but "you" are not who you think you are.


You are not your personality, you are not your thoughts or achievements,
and you are not your perceived success or failure.
In fact very little of "what you think you are" is truly you.

The "you" you think you are is an actor playing a role that your soul has chosen.


The real you is something far grander, far more expansive and far more amazing.
The real "you" is the actor but it is also the author, director and producer of the show.
Your soul is the executive producer – it rules the show.


Therefore, remember that your life is a journey that your soul has chosen.
All you need to do is play the part well. Keep an open heart and mind.
Sooner or later you will realise that there is a higher force
constantly guiding you.


That higher force is not outside of you.

It is inside you. *It is the real you.*

*Your potential* is your destiny waiting to be fulfilled
Just as the oak tree already exists within its seed
So too the story of your life and all the characters that play a part in it
already existed prior to you being born

*Every* seemingly trivial thought or event in your life has relevance. All has purpose and meaning, even if you don't immediately see it. Everything you experience today whether consciously or otherwise, you will process in your dream state tonight. As you dream, your subconscious mind flicks through the day's events as if replaying a movie. It connects today's experiences to your past experiences, all that you have experienced both in this life and in past lives. Your soul processes and sorts through all the data and then files each experience or impression into its appropriate section. Bits of information come together like the pieces of a puzzle to build the picture of your life. Every experience helps you to realise more about you. Each moment you are collecting and storing information that forms the bigger picture. As the bits fit together you begin to better understand your life and will come to see that everything serves a purpose.

*Love* is the only thing truly present in your heart

Embrace and accept the positive and negative aspects of yourself

And you will expand your understanding of love

If you try to disown the parts of you that you don't like

The things you try to deny will haunt and confront you

until you love them

When you love and accept the things you don't like about you

The things you don't like will automatically transform

You may not have the power to change the world

But you have the power to change your perception of it

In the heart of love,
all unites and becomes one
Through an eternal moment
time was born
And created the space of light
where your truth dwells
The eternal fire of love
A golden arrow pierced your heart
And you bled a crimson river
that fills your night
with longing
The heart of love
came to lift the veil
and a secret was revealed
A timeless truth
that transformed you
even as it created you
A tree of love
whose branches reach the heavens
And whose roots penetrate
deep within the Earth
Express the love you feel
in your heart
For it is the greatest contribution
you can ever make to the world
Keep an open heart
and you will feel something beautiful
Something inspirational
that stems
from the heart of love

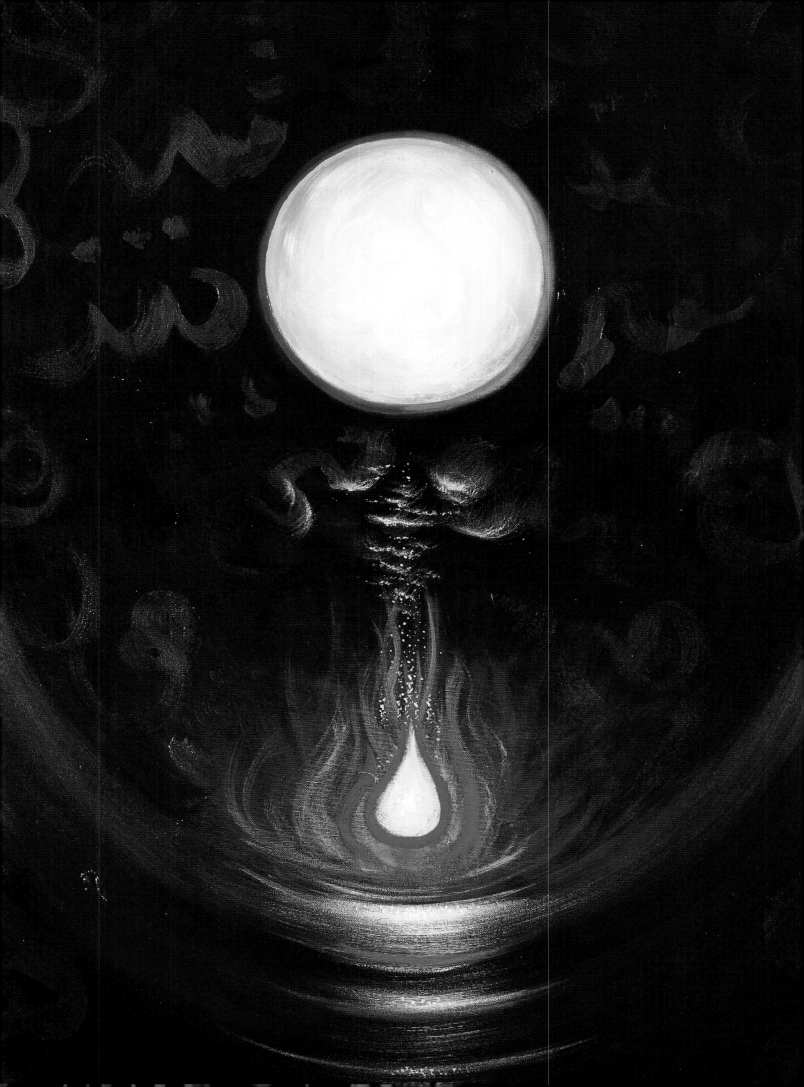

At some point, far back in time, our Earth had not yet been
formed, nor had the planets and stars that surround us.
Imagine in your mind's eye, this beautiful blue sphere being
formed by stardust — imagine the original point of creation
from which we stem.

---

The universe spans trillions of light years in every direction
and is continually expanding.
Our galaxy alone contains about one hundred billion stars
and recent estimates suggest that the number of galaxies
in the observable universe may be as high as one hundred
billion. Pause for a moment and reflect on how amazing
that is.

**There** is nothing you need to prove or achieve,
just let the river carry you.
Jump in just as you are
with all the light and dark aspects of your nature.
The positive and negative, the beautiful and ugly,
the shadow self and the radiant being,
all these are a part of you and all are worthy of love.
Let them all take the journey.

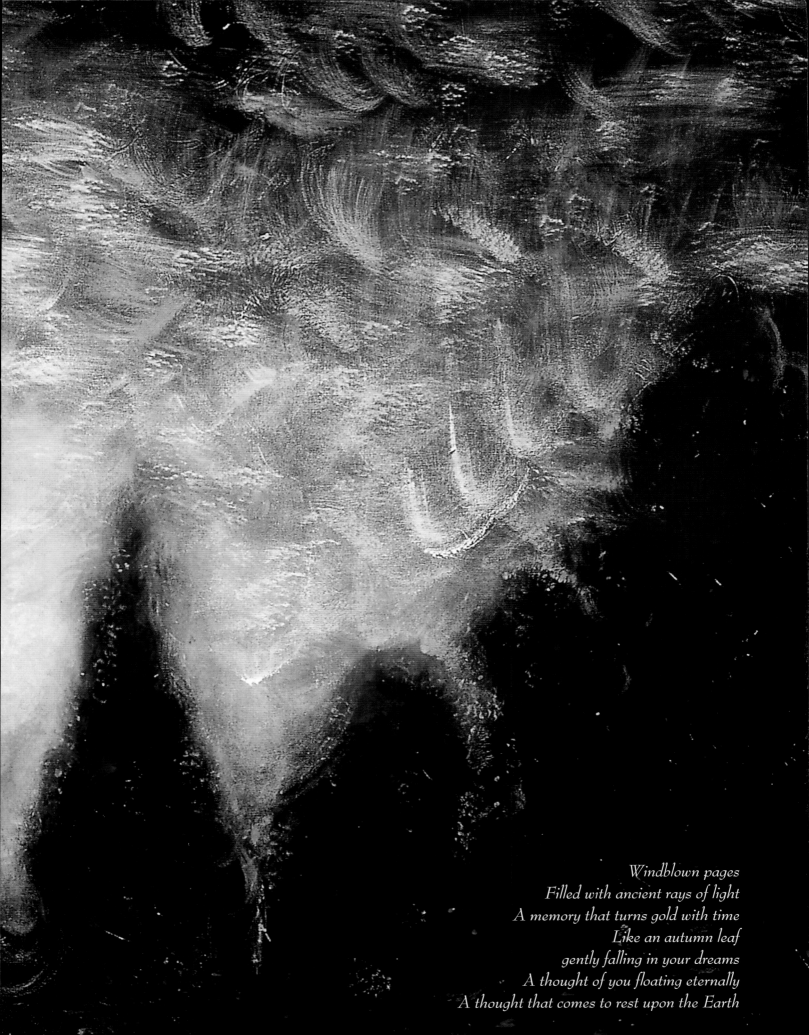

*Windblown pages*
*Filled with ancient rays of light*
*A memory that turns gold with time*
*Like an autumn leaf*
*gently falling in your dreams*
*A thought of you floating eternally*
*A thought that comes to rest upon the Earth*

# Embrace

life's ever-changing seasons
with acceptance and trust
For all in life is forever changing
in accordance with nature's divine will
Through endless cycles
of love and pain
we all eventually surrender
Graciously letting go
all that no longer serves our highest good
in the knowing that nothing is ever truly lost
for all exists eternally within
the universal heart

## A Great Spirit

tells her story
Set within a cosmic ocean of love
A jewel in a sphere of dreams
Blessed by the emerald dew that formed the Earth
Her love is an invisible shield that reflects light
Each new day her path leads us closer to the Sun
A sacred journey through war and peace
Step into her void and you will discover her mystery
Through the unknown she gives birth
She shapes all that is yet unformed
Her will is your destiny
Love it and an infinite pool of possibility will unfold
She lives inside your heart
In a place where all is possible
Her story is your story

*True* wisdom is an invisible light
you hold within you.
It is a guiding light,
the love which emanates from your soul.
This loving guidance is felt
through feeling and intuition –
pay attention to it
and you will discover new things,
new ways of looking at life.
Look silently, deeply and truthfully.
Eventually you will realise
that true wisdom is simply love –
an unconditional love
that is all around you.

Help me to see
that which cannot see,
help me to love
that which I do not love,
help me to find
that which I have lost,
help me to set free
all I have imprisoned.

# Night Wind
♡

One day I will return to you
   flowing on the wind from whence
  I have come –
on a teardrop – to the centre of
  your heart –

Beloved – with a deeper understanding
    I return – after eons of time
through countless cycles of love
   and pain – joy and sorrow –

My heart both broken and strengthened
    by love
Looking like an empty sea –
I listen to the rain, I feel my
heart beat in the silence of the
   night
I feel the wind blow through my
    heart and it clears my
   mind and I dream of long ago
in a beautiful garden in heaven –
when god and goddess wept
   tears of joy upon the earth –
Memories – flowing like a river –
    like the night wind
that blows as it waits for
the sun to rise –
   with an eternally loving heart
♡

# The rational

mind doesn't believe that something can exist unless it has a beginning and an end. We believe that we exist in a concrete, finite world that is governed by time and space, yet this perception is an illusion. In actuality we are part of a multidimensional reality that is infinite and truly magnificent. Yet this multidimensional reality is beyond the perception of our human mind and therefore beyond our logical understanding. From our human perspective things are born and then die, things begin then end, things function then stop functioning. On the surface this is how it appears to us. However, when scientists delve deep into the microscopic, sub-atomic world a completely different picture emerges. Energetically nothing ever actually dies or ends, it simply changes from one form to another.

All of life is essentially one. We are each energetically interconnected with one another and with everything around us. Everything we experience is in a way a part of ourselves being reflected back to us. To truly master life is to understand that in essence everyone and everything is part of you.

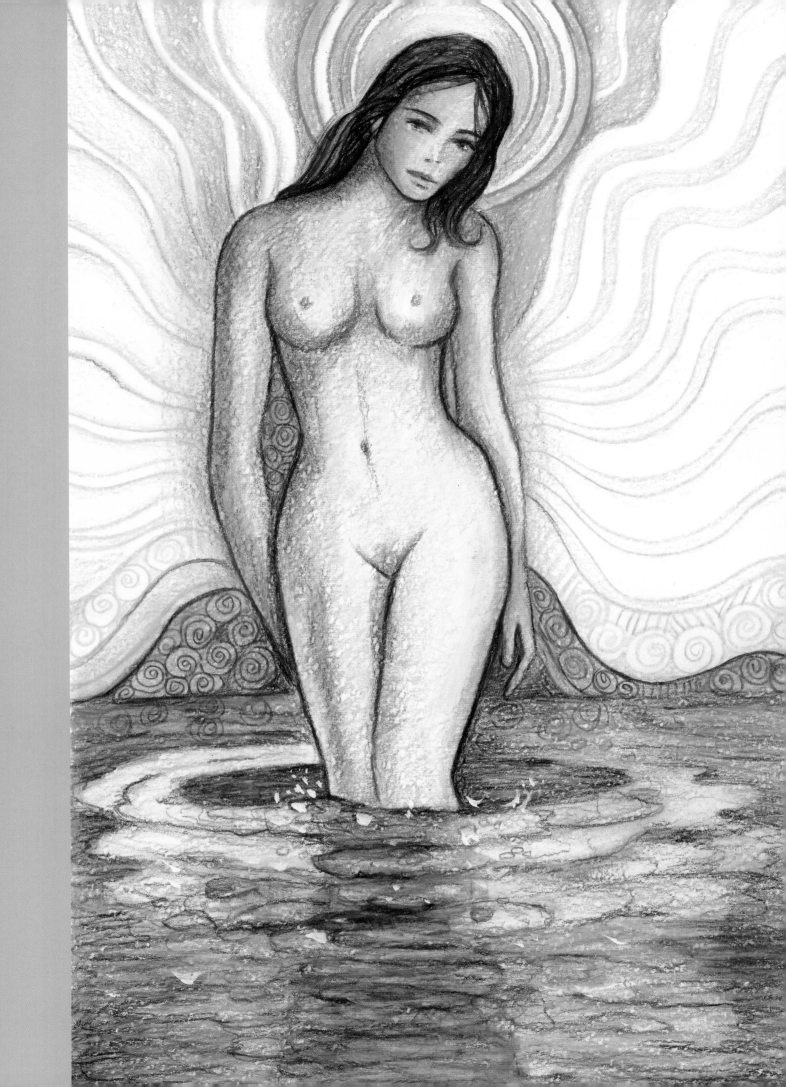

... known ... were ... in ...

In joy of love and life forever it will be the light will ... there is but one love one flame one heart and all else ... one heart so I say to you be still and join me - and you ... ever will be ... the light of truth, you will come to see as ... you will find me ... tear drops from heaven ... my flame eternally mine ... want you to remember my ... and we share the sparkling sky ... see all the wonder in the ... see you ... in the pink flame that shines through you ... our eternal hearts be ... holy spirit of love and ... the world, the flowering of life ... see all life for what ... the loving heart within is all ... come you in song ... feel the ... with the sun, see the ... and sing you ... know I have always loved you ... it has always been so that I have always loved ... being ... to come to you ... through you ... and forever it is ... you are now ... still and ... peace ...

Imagination
makes the
invisible world
visible

———————

Great things
are possible
if what you do
aligns with your
heartfelt purpose
and vision

You do not need to
protect yourself from others
As much as you need to
protect yourself from
your own negativity and fears

You are, in essence, light
An ocean reflecting the light of an inner sun
A universe through which all in the universe responds
A star through which new stars are born
An eternal heart through which we all experience love

# Wisdom

*is the light of the soul*
*It is the love and acceptance*
*of all there is*
*as it is*
*So begin by*
*loving and accepting yourself*
*as you are*

I am like a forgotten memory buried deep within your heart
I am an ocean of scattered feelings drifting to the shore
I am the windblown pages of ancient days and moonlit nights
I am an autumn leaf drifting through your dreams,
High above the world
Brighter than the Sun

# TREE MEDITATION

Imagine yourself in a magic forest, walking along a path on a cool still evening. All around you is glowing with moonlight. You are surrounded by an array of majestic trees as you feel the cool night air as a gentle breeze caressing your face and skin. You are alone, yet you feel completely safe and secure as you walk along this magical path. You feel a deep spiritual connection to the Earth and trees. The path leads you to a mysterious old door at the base of a huge old tree. You stand before this majestic tree, in awe of its beauty… feel its strength, its wisdom and love pouring down upon you through the starlight.

Open the door and step inside. The room is glowing, a deep green and violet light fills the room and you feel these colours heal you. Feel the green and violet light heal and transmute all past hurts and fears. All your secret fears, doubts, jealousy, repressed anger, sadness and regret energetically detach from you and ignite as sparks consumed by the violet light and healed by the deep green light. Your entire being is engulfed by violet and deep green flames of light as you begin to feel a deep sense of peace – feeling lighter and brighter, feeling renewed, physically, emotionally and spiritually, as though an invisible weight has been removed.

You now realise that this sacred tree is your higher self, your spiritual guardian – and everything you have ever experienced is stored here.

Your life experiences are held lovingly within the many corridors and rooms. There are many doors to many rooms, many stairs and levels within your sacred tree, all filled with the treasures and experiences of your life. You are free now to walk around and explore the sacred rooms and walkways within your tree of life.

Ask your higher self now to show you something that would be of help to you at this point in your life. What would it take for you to remain happy and free? Ask to be shown to a particular room that would be of help, or be an inspiration to you.

Now thank your sacred tree – your higher self – for appearing to you in this way and for helping you during this meditation. Know that you may return here any time you like.

Slowly bring your awareness back to your breath – become aware of your physical body and open your eyes when you are ready.

*Believe in yourself*
for you are a wonder of creation.
Let go of fear and you'll discover a shining star.
Trust in the healing power of love.
You are an ocean of light,
Reflecting the light of the Sun, universe and stars.
Love's flame resides in your heart,
And through this love new stars are born.
Through an explosion of love
Your glowing heart moves the ocean's tide
One eternal heart forever

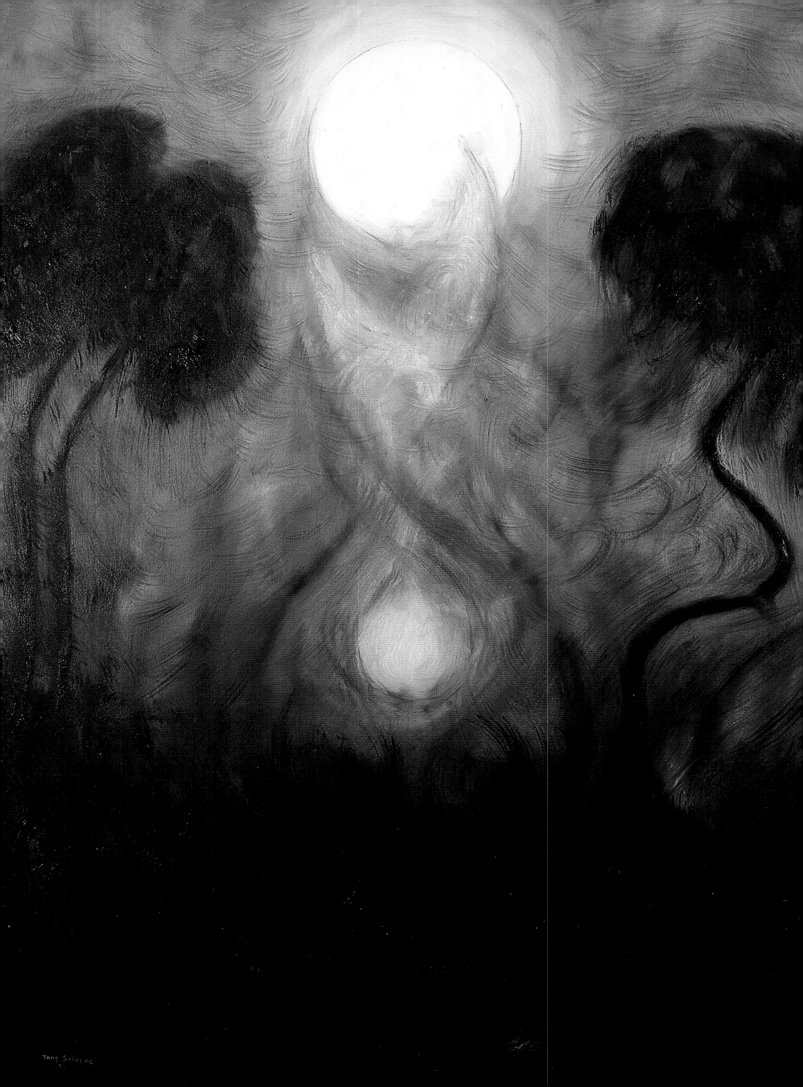

*At* some point every soul leaves this Earth
To travel beyond the horizon of time
Through the ancient mists of our collective imagination
We journey back towards infinity
To a point of light with no beginning or end
And rest upon the tranquil shore of creation
We bathe in its turquoise sea,
a sea of love, until we melt
In an ocean of light
A pause in eternity
Far away from time
Until Spirit calls and asks us to return.
And so the cycle continues,
through the invisible wheel that moves the earth and stars
We are reborn into this earthly realm
But we do not remember what came before
Until we feel a stirring in our hearts
And realise that the past, present and future are one

*Before we know it* we shall return to the great void of creation from whence we have come.

*We are the light of soul within the eternal glow of spirit.*

*Through a maze of mixed emotions our souls shall flow, through the haze and fog of this world,*
*until we each find the clear crystal path of peace which leads to the great ocean of love.*

*On our way, we shall remember that all our learning was simply recollection,*
*every piece of knowledge and wisdom was already inside us.*

*Even before the stars were born, the greatest wisdom lay in the space between a word and thought.*

*I feel peace; there is a vast space in my soul.*

*I gaze at the sky and I become the sky.*

*Thinking of miracles,*
*I realise what a miracle this life is.*

*Emptiness is life's potential waiting to be filled.*

*A ray of light fills my heart and a universe unfolds from within the light.*

*I feel Gaia, this beautiful planet Earth.*

*I feel rivers branching out, flowing through my body, my mind and soul;*

*I see rivers flowing out streams of dreams.*

*There are many colours inside my heart, colours that smell of earth and soil. Colours that smell like trees,*
*that remind me of dew drops in the morning, and lush green grass, and meadows — deserts —*
*rain and sunshine — clouds — flowers, jasmine and jonquils — roses and purple crystals.*

*A greater universe flows out from a smaller one.*

*I create memories, veils, illusions. I use mirrors, I replicate.*

*One must go beyond time to discover the present.*

*There is a place where love is real.*

*Gazing at the sky I realise how important love is.*

*A tear flows into my heart.*

*As you read these words, my soul flows out through the spaces.*

*Future generations, our children and their children will know your words also.*

*They will know you as I know you now.*

*I project myself into the future through the soul of words, through you who reads them.*

*Life is a circle of interconnected souls, driven by a great invisible wheel, a great invisible will.*

*And yet that will is visible in Gaia and her impeccable nature, it is visible through the changing seasons and through the cycles of life — birth, death and rebirth.*

*Behind this mask, behind every mask, there is only love.*

*I shall love you in your dreams.*

*Together we shall drift beyond the horizon of time.*

*We shall gaze into each other's soul.*

*Through ancient mists we shall travel and sleep.*

*We shall awaken within a womb where another life begins, always within the same circle.*

*A thought of you I will carry in my heart,
a thought that shall grow to be an ocean that forever longs for you.*

*Until I find you, until we meet again my soul shall ebb and flow between our shores,
my soul shall burn the eternal flame.*

*Your memory casts a tapestry of rainbow light upon my soul.*

*We are each rays of love, and yet we shall not remember but for the stirring within our hearts —
a new day full of beautiful things — a new Earth — a new heaven.*

*Life has no reason but love.*

*How grateful I am to have known you.*

*Gaia, Earth Goddess, Divine Mother, forever present inside us,
from within your sacred heart many future Earths and stars shall be born.*

*And from within those Earths and stars, other Earths and stars shall be born for you are a seed of creation.*

*May each of us be blessed and be healed,
may we each have the compassion, strength and courage to be like you.*

*You are the gateway to an endless universe. Engulf me with your blue and emerald light.*

*Through time a miracle unfolds.
Through you I feel the wind — I become the wind and caress each leaf of grass.*

*I am a beautiful oak tree that watches the stars at night,*
*through endless summers, autumns, winters and springs, I penetrate deeper into your heart.*

*Dearest Gaia, I feel the pounding of your ocean inside my heart.*

*Forever I have loved you.*

*You are all that is beautiful in our world,*
*the embodiment of the love and wisdom of every age and culture,*
*forever reflecting all that is sacred.*

*In you I see the hidden parts of myself;*
*I discover my soul and intuitively come to know the secret meaning of the stars.*

*Reflected in you is my own reflection.*

*Aware of my soul, you are the gateway to my soul.*

*In my soul, time and space contain past, present and future; nothing is lost.*

*The future contains a thousand violet suns, I move freely between Heaven and Earth,*
*through endless dimensions and realities.*

*Time is still and yet life is constantly in motion,*
*a creation beyond our understanding and ultimately formless.*

*Life is like water flowing through a stream.*

*My heart is an ocean of light; our lives a beautiful tapestry,*
*every thread forms part of the overall beauty, every thread has its own story.*

*Within the bigger picture there is no one specific place or purpose;*
*and yet all is an integral part of the whole.*

*So it is that 'we — humanity' are each unique, we make this world what it is,*
*a beautiful tapestry called Gaia.*

*Gently close your eyes and relax. Let each muscle and joint relax, let go of any tension*
*and bring your focus to your breath.*

*As you breathe in, breathe in my love, and breathe in the love of the universe.*

*I am Gaia*

*Breathe in my healing light;*
*and in return, share with me your vast and unconditional love.*

## About the artist and author

**TONI CARMINE SALERNO** is an internationally recognised bestselling author and artist. Through his work which transcends cultures and borders, he explores universal and timeless themes such as spirituality, poetry, philosophy and love. His paintings are collected by people from around the globe and his publications are available in over 15 languages.

Toni's artwork is infused with a soulful healing energy that helps us to connect to our spiritual selves; they are meditations in paint and colour that guide us to an infinite source of love and wisdom that we each hold within. His work continues to quietly illuminate hearts and minds around the globe.

For more information on Toni's work, please visit the following websites:
**www.tonicarminesalerno.com**
**www.blueangelonline.com**

*Also by Toni Carmine Salerno*

ORACLE CARDS:
*Universal Love*
*Universal Wisdom*
*Spirit Oracle*
*Lovers Oracle*
*Guardian Angel Cards*
*Crystal Oracle*
*Angels, Gods & Goddesses*
*Magdalene Oracle*
*Ask An Angel*
*Gaia Oracle*
*Healing Angel Cards*
*Soul Mate Cards*
*Blue Angel Oracle*
*Heart and Soul Cards*
*Wisdom of the Golden Path*

BOOKS:
*Jewels Within A Teardrop*
*Toni Carmine Salerno: Art, Life, Reflections*
*Angelic Inspirations*
*Goddess: The Eternal Feminine within Life & Nature*

CDs:
*Meditations For Inner Peace*
*Meditations For Children (with Elizabeth Beyer)*
*Heart Meditations (with Martine Salerno)*

For more information on Blue Angel Publishing
or any of our releases, please visit our website at:

*www.blueangelonline.com*